Patient Watching

by

Judith Wozniak

First published 2022 by The Hedgehog Poetry Press

Published in the UK by
The Hedgehog Poetry Press
5, Coppack House
Churchill Avenue
Clevedon
BS21 6QW

www.hedgehogpress.co.uk

ISBN: 978-1-913499-76-1

For Ted

A doctor writes a poem in the chart,
though none can read its invisible lines,
or understand the mystery of death.

- Rafael Campo

Contents

A FORTUNATE MAN

After John Berger

I feel the heat of her gaze on my face
as I palpate the mound of her belly,
listen in, look up and catch a flicker
of a smile. She knows before I speak
her baby is not a breech this time.
I check, balloting the smooth head under
my fingers, trace the curve of the spine.
Silence crackles with the unspoken

the baby she lost. A farmer's wife,
she understands some things are not meant
to be. Then the ripple, a quickening,
we both thrill at the nudge of a foot.

As I help her up, she squeezes my hand,
I have cared for her since she was a child.

*

I have cared for her since she was a child,
watch as she caps her baby's head
in the crook of her arm, smooths down
silk-spun curls, lulls with soft sounds.

I unwrap him, swaddled in his shawl,
blow on the bell of my stethoscope
in the scoop of my hand, take off the chill.
He grasps my finger in his dimpled fist.

I lift him, nested in his mother's lap,
high up, sense how his legs stiffen,
scissor, step the air, his toes point.
I need to choose the right moment
to warn her he may struggle to walk.
All I can do now is watch and wait

*

All I can do now is watch and wait.
I linger in the doorway, glance back,
I think this may be for the last time,
my shadow has already taken leave.

This man is more than my patient.
We often spend evenings sat together
in comfortable silence, nursing a beer.
I hoped we would age together.

A clatter downstairs from the kitchen,
his wife still baking treats to tempt him,
keeping busy in a bubble of denial.
I promise him I will check on her

afterwards, for now I need to ensure
my friend has all the care he needs.

*

I worry she has all the care she needs.
Her son, still wearing his father's old suit,
removes the oversized cap that rests
on his ears, rolls it in calloused hands
grimed with soil, anxiously greets me
when I call on his elderly mother
confined to her bed. The nurses say
he can be a bit rough with the hoist,

so I make sure I see her alone,
ask her is if she is well looked after.
She clutches my hand and tells me
not to worry, he is a good boy,
he keeps her *neat as a bandbox*.
I stay vigilant so nothing is missed.

*

I stay vigilant so nothing is missed.
Sometimes all I can do is listen.
She tells my wife she needs to see me
again, today, that I will understand.

Each time another new symptom
—nothing ever hangs together.
She sits on the edge of her seat
biting her lip, knitting her hands.

Neither of us will be satisfied
at the end of the consultation.
There will never be enough time
to iron out her disappointments.

I tell her there is nothing to find.
I know it's not what she wants to hear.

*

I know it's not what she wants to hear.
Most weeks I visit her husband at home.
Tied to the sigh of the oxygen cylinder,
he struggles to heave breath into stiff lungs.
Trapped in his armchair, his thinned skin
sheds silvered flakes, fine as moths' wings.
His cough erupts like bubbles through mud,
he hides froths of sputum in a lidded pot.

I don't often I see her in surgery alone.
After I examine her, she sits on the couch,
stares at the floor, dangles her wasted legs,
listens to what I have to say, hoping
her referral to the specialist can wait.
I notice just how much she has changed.

*

I notice just how much she has changed
in her short red kilt, the black-clad
spider legs. How brittle she is,
slumped in a chair or pacing the room.

And then it begins — I watch her
spiral down as her props fall away.
Her fingers tremble, scatter ash
into shrivelled pots of geraniums.

The garden, a tangle of weeds,
borders choked with brambles.
Bruised windfalls, worried by wasps,
rot neglected in the parched grass.

I should have noticed sooner.
This happens on my watch.

*

This happens on my watch.
They are already gathered outside
when I arrive. I join in the search
over the meadow, a fan of beams

flicks up over the trees. We push
on through the long dry grass,
reach the river slicked with oil.
A solitary bouquet fades on a bush.

In the water a hunched shape.
My torch lights up a tree trunk
silvered by the moon. I peer in,
the hazed reflection is mine.

A shout— I'm relieved he's safe.
It's not what I expected to find.

*

It's not what I expected to find.
A call for young Rosie with abdominal pain,

bent over the kitchen table clutching her back,
the dogs yapping and worrying at my ankles.

I examine her under layers of baggy clothes.
She is in labour. I break the news to her mother

who wears her 'load of nonsense' expression.
No, not my Rosie. She's going to college.

The midwife arrives in time, takes charge
comfortingly upholstered into her uniform.

I worry when Rosie won't hold her baby,
but her mum coaxes the small bundle between them

until Rosie holds her and names her Marjorie.
You never know anything for certain.

*

You never know anything for certain.
Elsie had cared for her sister for decades.
I discover a secret sat between them.
The daughter her sister would never discuss,
her 'disgrace', taken from her at birth.
Every night, one each side of the hearth,
they hoarded the past until for one of them
it became a trickle of memory.

She shows me a crumpled letter tucked
in the pocket of her pleated tweed skirt.
It's from her niece. Elsie has been in touch
with her for years. Now her sister has died
should she meet her, try to make amends?
They trust me with their secrets and fears.

*

They trust me with their secrets and fears.
Her husband twists his wedding ring,

she balls a damp hankie in her fist
tries to order her tumble of worries.

It's their grandson. They took him in
when his parents could no longer cope.

He shouts at them, shuts himself away,
she knows he steals from her purse.

Last night he smashed up his room
they are frightened to be alone with him.

I have tried to get this troubled lad help
for years. Sometimes it takes a crisis.

I have already been told what happened.
I rely on this tight-knit community.

*

I rely on this tight-knit community.
Out on my rounds, I often see Flo
her sparse curls squashed under a hairnet.

The sun tidemark where nut-brown arms
meet her rolled up sleeves. Hinged forward
she hurries as if trying to catch herself up.

Busy delivering; a box of newly laid eggs
warm from her hens, pots of damson jam,
plump tomatoes in a twist of paper

left on doorsteps of the newly bereaved,
the housebound. Her seesaw gait is worse,
she needs a new hip but refuses to leave

her mother's ashes, buried on her land.
I know all they had was each other.

*

I know all they have is each other.
My tyres crunch over frosted gravel,
along an unmade track I know so well.
A fox startles in the beam of headlights
as my jeep rolls across a rut in the road.
Her husband waits at the end of the path,
an old jacket pulled over his pyjamas,
hair tangled from another restless sleep.
He stands too close, questions spill over,
every detail rehearsed while he waited.
We climb upstairs to a solitary light.
I check, talk to her all the while, though
she has already slipped away, I will stay
with them both, in the quiet of the night.

*

She waits up in the quiet of the night.
Sometimes I sit outside, watch the light
change. I glimpse her in the corner
of my mind's eye, it's enough she's there.

I witness how my patients struggle,
watch how their stories unfold
in the melt of time. Share with them
lived moments of joy and sorrow.

Soaking up the suffering of others
can tip me into despair. She listens.
I think anguish has its own timescale,
so, I work harder to run ahead of death.

I need these people as they need me
and count myself a fortunate man.

*

I have cared for some since childhood.
Often all I can do is watch and wait,
ensure they have the care they need.

I stay vigilant so nothing is missed,
notice when they change. Sometimes
tell them what they don't want to hear.

I learn from what happens on my watch,
it's not always what I expect to find.
You never know anything for certain.

They trust me with their secrets and fears
I rely on this tight-knit community,
we know— all we have is each other.

I think of them in the quiet of the night
and count myself a fortunate man.

*

PATTERN RECOGNITION

All I can do is watch
from the edge of things,
pressed against the cool tiled wall
in my white coat with a blue flash —
allowed only to observe.
They crash through bendy doors
from the ambulance bay,
a man brought in on a blue light,
outrunners in green scrubs,
masks slung under their chins,
scoot the trolley along the corridor —
a clatter of white clogs.
I watch them
tap the back of his hand,
hunt for a vein,
cut away his clothes,
shave some chest hair
to help the electrodes stick.
His skin slicked with sweat,
pale as damp dough.
I know this look.

I have seen this look —
pale as damp dough,
slicked with sweat,
his shirt stuck to his chest.
She loosens his tie,
worries at the buttons.
I didn't know he was hairy.
The doctor holds his wrist.
listens to his chest.
I watch them.

He is slumped in the chair.
Blue lights pulse the ceiling,
the front door wide open,
men in shiny black shoes
standing in the hallway —
the crackle of a radio.
I know I have to be still,
shiver in my nightie,
pressed against the Anaglypta
on the edge of things.
All I can do is watch.

INVISIBLE

Nobody notices your trousers concertina round your feet, that you keep having to hitch them up to meet the pale moon of skin beneath your school t-shirt.

Nobody feels able to hug you. If they did they would feel the hollows crumple between your ribs, your twig thin arms.

Nobody remarks how often you fall asleep on your desk cradled in the crook of your elbow, dark circles etched round your eyes.

Nobody watches you shuffle round the playground clinging on to your loose scuffed shoes with your toes.

Nobody pats your head, feels the stiffness of your uncombed hair.

Nobody stops to wonder if anyone shampoos it in the bath, makes soap spikes stick up to make you laugh, scoops warm water over your head taking care not to sting your eyes.

Nobody knows you only have half a sandwich in a carrier bag, you don't have a lunch box with secret pockets for surprise snacks.

Nobody sees you snaffle left over scraps, discarded apple cores, hoping to find a crust with a smear of peanut butter.

Nobody worries you walk home alone, shivering in your thin coat, kicking the leaves, taking your time because you know

Nobody is there for you.

SATURDAY MORNING EMERGENCY SURGERY

He walked from the city through the night,
sheltered under a hedge in the front garden
of his family home.

He smells sour from sleeping rough
for weeks. His hair raked into runnels
with his fingers. Broken boots, no socks.

He weeps on my shoulder, as tall now
as my own son. Too old for foster care,
not ill enough to be admitted.

I persuade him to let me phone his Mum,
to beg for a short respite, make a plan.
She sobs, I know she can't take any more.

I find him a hostel back in the city,
tuck money and the biscuits from reception
in the frayed pocket of his great coat.

It is not enough.
I know it is not enough.

DISCLOSURE

Sometimes I just have to wait
in the thick silence of a held breath
and hope the phone won't ring,
that nobody knocks with coffee,
aware of the echo of children
playing in the school nearby.

Resist a glance at my watch,
try not to pierce the stillness
everything else can wait
what I say next will matter.

...

A letter arrives the next day
delivered by hand marked
'Private and Confidential'.

She says she is so sorry,
it's her fault, she misled me.
She thinks I must have noticed

the smudge on her cheek
covered up with make-up.
At home they all know

how clumsy she can be.
She asks me not to reply.

...

I am driven to the safe house
through a puzzle of back streets.
A wary greeting from women
stood tight together holding
babes in arms. It's a school day.

I am there to talk to them,
first I listen to their stories:
they are angry with doctors
I learn the power of *sorry*.

I don't recognise her at first
sitting alone at the back.

HOLDING A STRANGER

I stay with the stranger lying in the road
in a pool of light from the streetlamp.
He has a pulse, I feel the brush of his breath
as I lean in close to ask his name. Shout out.
There's nobody around— he's slipping away
I think he says *don't leave me.*

It begins to snow, I cover him with my coat,
fumble my frosted fingers to call for help.
I shout again. Across the street a torch
flicks on, curtains move, then darkness.

Is this how it was for you that night?
Did somebody hold you, ask your name
or turn out the light, leave it to another
to find you when it was too late.

ACKNOWLEDGEMENTS

I would like to thank the inspirational tutors on the MA course, Tamar Yoseloff and Glyn Maxwell and all the poets in my group. Thanks also to Roger Bloor, Diana Cant, Vanessa Lampert and Mary Mulholland for their helpful feedback on these poems, my husband Ted for his trusty red pen, and Mark Davidson at the Hedgehog Press.